FEEDING THE FIRE

FEEDING THE FIRE

POEMS
Jeffrey Harrison

*For Nancy —
with good wishes for
your poems. At The
Frost Place.*

SARABANDE BOOKS
LOUISVILLE, KENTUCKY

Managing Editor
Sarabande Books, Inc.
2234 Dundee Road, Suite 200
Louisville, KY 40205

Library of Congress Cataloging-in-Publication Data

Harrison, Jeffrey.
Feeding the fire : poems / by Jeffrey Harrison.
    p.   cm.
    ISBN 1-889330-63-9 (cloth : alk. paper) —
ISBN 1-889330-64-7 (pbk. : alk. paper)
I. Title.
PS 3558.A67133 F44 2001
811'.54—dc21   2001020183

Cover painting: *Harbor, Monhegan*, by James Wyeth © 1998. Used by kind permission of the artist.

Cover and text design by Charles Casey Martin

Manufactured in the United States of America
This book is printed on acid-free paper.

Sarabande Books is a nonprofit literary organization.

Funded in part by a grant from the Kentucky Arts Council, a state agency of the Education, Arts and Humanities Cabinet, and by a grant from the National Endowment for the Arts.

FIRST EDITION

for Charlie Worthen

Contents

III

Acknowledgments

I am grateful to the John Simon Guggenheim Memorial Foundation for a fellowship which enabled me to complete this collection; to Phillips Academy for my term as Roger Murray Writer-in-Residence, during which some of these poems were written; to Karen Chase, Theodore Deppe, Jessica Greenbaum, Eric Karpeles, Francesco Rognoni, William Wenthe, Charlie Worthen, and especially Robert Cording, Peter Schmitt, and Baron Wormser, for their helpful suggestions about the poems and manuscript; to Colleen Mohyde for her good-natured assistance; and to Julie, always the first reader of these poems.

Grateful acknowledgment is made to the editors of the following publications in which these poems first appeared, sometimes in slightly different form:

The Acre: "Not Written on Birch Bark"
Chelsea: "Golden Retriever," "Interval"
DoubleTake: "Salt"
The Gettysburg Review: "Masturbation"
The Hudson Review: "White Spaces"
Iron Horse Literary Review: "Another Story," "Three Wishes"
The Kenyon Review: "Horseshoe Contest"
Meridian: "The Burning Hat" (as "Early Loss")
Michigan Quarterly Review: "The Diver"
The New Republic: "Rilke's Fear of Dogs"

The Paris Review: "A Garbage Can in Brooklyn Full of Books,"
"Remembered Departure"

Ploughshares: "Necessity," "The Pond of Desires"

Poetry: "My Double Nonconversion"

Poetry Kanto: "Wherever You Are"

The Recorder: "Figure," "Medusa"

Seneca Review: "Vietnam Scrapbook"

Shenandoah: "Green Canoe"

The Southern Review: "Our Other Sister," "Oval Pin," "Time
Smear"

Tar River Poetry: "Arrangement," "The Cardinal Flower"

TriQuarterly: "Smoke Follows Beauty"

Western Humanities Review: "Lure"

The Yale Review: "Family Dog," "Rowing," "Sex and Poetry"

The New Bread Loaf Anthology of Contemporary American Poetry,
edited by Michael Collier and Stanley Plumly: "Arrangement,"
"Family Dog"

Poetry: An Introduction, third edition, and *The Bedford Introduction to
Literature*, sixth edition, by Michael Meyer: "Horseshoe Contest"

"Rowing" won the Poetry Society of America's Lyric Poem Award.

"The Diver" won The Loft's Poetry Prize.

The Bachelard quotation is from *Fragments of A Poetics of Fire*, by Gaston Bachelard, edited by Suzanne Bachelard and translated by Kenneth Haltman (The Dallas Institute Publications, 1990).

The Williams quotation is from *The Selected Poems of William Carlos Williams*, (New Directions, 1969).

The Kafka quotation is from *Conversations with Kafka*, by Gustav Janouch, translated by Goronwy Rees (New Directions, 1971).

Memory catches fire; the poet tends the blaze,
breathing the embers to life.
                                —Gaston Bachelard

Their time past, pulled down
cracked and flung to the fire
                        —William Carlos Williams

What one writes is merely the ashes of one's experience.
                        —Franz Kafka

I

GREEN CANOE

I don't often get the chance any longer
to go out alone in the green canoe
and, lying in the bottom of the boat,
just drift where the breeze takes me,
down to the other end of the lake
or into some cove without my knowing
because I can't see anything over
the gunwales but sky as I lie there,
feeling the ribs of the boat as my own,
this floating pod with a body inside it . . .

also a mind, that drifts among clouds
and the sounds that carry over water—
a flutter of birdsong, a screen door
slamming shut—as well as the usual stuff
that clutters it, but slowed down, opened up,
like the fluff of milkweed tugged
from its husk and floating over the lake,
to be mistaken for mayflies at dusk
by feeding trout, or be carried away
to a place where the seeds might sprout.

LURE

"What a sexy name for a piece of fishing gear,"
said Mrs. Stevens. At nine or ten
I wasn't old enough to know what she meant.
I was casting a Phoebe Wobbler or a Daredevil
off the end of the dock, and I wasn't
getting any strikes. Blonde hair pulled back,
a few wisps of it falling across her forehead,
high cheekbones, long sun-tanned legs
beneath her short tennis skirt—these were things
I didn't pay much attention to back then
and remember dimly, as if they were underwater.
She was probably ten years younger
than I am now. I couldn't understand
why she was making such a big deal
about a word. I just kept casting
and reeling in the clear line, pushing and releasing
the button on my Zebco. I didn't even have to pretend
I didn't catch on, and it never got weird
being alone with her down there on the dock.
The waters of adulthood were unfathomable,
though I sensed in the clinking drinks
and cocktail laughter of my parents and their friends
something silvery flashing under the surface.
Mrs. Stevens could have been up to anything
or nothing. Maybe she was just practicing

her grown-up talk, or maybe she was flirting,
testing me. Maybe she already knew
she was going to leave her husband in a few years,
listing among her reasons that he wasn't good enough
at tennis. He already had the sad eyes
of a dog who'd been abandoned by the highway.
I saw him ten years later, when I was in college,
sitting alone in one of those bars with lobster traps
and trophy fish on the walls, fishing nets
draped from the ceiling. After our surprised hellos,
neither of us found much to say, and as I stood there
trying not to look into his bereft face,
I thought of how sexy his ex-wife used to be
and what it was like to be a kid
intent on hooking brook trout or rainbows.

OUR OTHER SISTER

for Ellen

The cruelest thing I did to my younger sister
wasn't shooting a homemade blowdart into her knee,
where it dangled for a breathless second

before dropping off, but telling her we had
another, older sister who'd gone away.
What my motives were I can't recall: a whim,

or was it some need of mine to toy with loss,
to probe the ache of imaginary wounds?
But that first sentence was like a strand of DNA

that replicated itself in coiling lies
when my sister began asking her desperate questions.
I called our older sister Isabel

and gave her hazel eyes and long blonde hair.
I had her run away to California
where she took drugs and made hippie jewelry.

Before I knew it, she'd moved to Santa Fe
and opened a shop. She sent a postcard
every year or so, but she'd stopped calling.

I can still see my younger sister staring at me,
her eyes widening with desolation
then filling with tears. I can still remember

how thrilled and horrified I was
that something I'd just made up
had that kind of power, and I can still feel

the blowdart of remorse stabbing me in the heart
as I rushed to tell her none of it was true.
But it was too late. Our other sister

had already taken shape, and we could not
call her back from her life far away
or tell her how badly we missed her.

FAMILY DOG

A succession of Newfoundlands
of diminishing nobility
and with names like English maids—
Flossie, Rosie, Nelly—
gave way, long after I'd left,
to this hyperactive black lab
who (like me?) never grew up,
always the exuberant puppy
to almost everyone's annoyance,
and whose name—Jess—is so much
like my own that when I'm home
and hear my father call the dog
or say his name in irritation
when he's gotten in the garbage
or chewed up someone's shoe,
I'm forced to relive an unpleasant
split second I lived many times
as a teenager, when my father
and I were chronic enemies—
a quick shock through my heart
and the thought, *Oh God, what
have I done now?* Followed now
by the realization, *It's only the dog,*
a sigh of relief, a quiet laugh. . . .
I'm almost always fooled,

as if the pitch of my father's voice
triggered some switch
in my nervous system, my body
still wired for sound
decades later, bringing back,
before I have time to think,
the fear, the rancor,
things I would rather forget,
the way a dog forgets
and always comes back, comes home
when his name is called,
knowing his master loves him.

MY DOUBLE NONCONVERSION

(NYC, 1976)

I must have been looking up at the stars
on the vaulted ceiling, that simulacrum of heaven,
as the muffled bustle of arrivals and departures
washed over me like surf. I must have looked
so young and unstreetwise in my wonder,
standing like that in Grand Central's concourse,
a perfect target for the skinhead in saffron robe
who greeted me and pushed into my hands
a garish edition of the *Bhagavad-Gita.*
And I must have been a very different person
from the one I later became, to stay
and talk with him, and even buy the book.

I'm trying to remember what it felt like
to be that person, a novitiate to the city
open to any approach. Less than a minute
after leaving the Hare Krishna, still inside
the basilical concourse, I allowed myself
to be waylaid by a young man with a Bible,
listened to the passages he quoted,
then (this is the part I can hardly believe)
knelt down with him in a bank of phone booths
and prayed, delirious with self-consciousness
as if God Himself were watching. Afterward,
he said a seed had been planted inside me.

That copy of the *Bhagavad-Gita* has slipped
into the gulf of twenty years between then and now,
and that seed has gone untended just as long.
When I left the Born-Again, I took the subway
uptown to Columbia, where I was a freshman,
then the dingy elevator up to my monklike cell:
one bed, one desk, one chair, one dresser, one window
facing a roofscape to the south, and open sky.
Also, a fern I'd bought my first day there
in front of St. John the Divine, from an old woman
who told me, with a look of crazed belief,
that someday it would grow into a tree.

TIME SMEAR

Julie's driving, I'm in the passenger seat
wearing holographic glasses that give the world
a prismatic aura as it all speeds by,
the Grateful Dead are playing on the stereo
for the first time in ages, and I feel
those ages rushing through me in reverse
until it's summer eighteen years ago.
We're on our way out to Colorado
to look for jobs, my brother Jeremy
in the back seat making peanut butter
and jelly sandwiches for lunch. We're just kids
though we don't think of it that way,
and the jobs we find will be just the kind of jolt
to our uncompleted college educations
we're looking for: Jeremy and I digging ditches
and planting trees in a soon-to-be-yet-another
golf course community, and Julie scooping
ice cream in Vail, a town so artificial
it's like a confection itself, a mall display
or children's board game surrounded by mountains.
Our boss, who lives there, is a smooth preener-type
we refer to as "Chip Ramsey, male prostitute."
I'm writing poems but would never dream
of putting him in one of them, or for that matter
the mobile home we've rented by the highway

where, at the end of the day, we drink beer and sit
really low on the couch so the bottom edge
of the picture window cuts the other trailers
out of the view and we just see mountains.
We're masquerading as the working class
and not quite pulling it off, knowing we'll be
out of there in a matter of weeks, but it feels good
to have jobs we can complain about and which,
for all three of us in fact, strengthen our arms.
But this is all a week or so away, we're still
driving out there, taking turns behind the wheel
of a French's-Mustard-colored AMC Hornet,
a truly crappy car that can barely catch its breath
on any kind of incline at higher altitudes.
Last night we slept on the bank of a river
wrapped in the thick cocoon of the rapids' roar,
and this morning we had rainbows for breakfast,
early sunlight haloing the leaping spray.
We don't need much, just the adrenalin
of driving is enough, the jittery hum
of sleeplessness in our veins, the slipping back
and forth between reflection and ecstasy
the Dead keep making happen, giving me
goose bumps now as they make their way between
"Not Fade Away" and "Going Down the Road

Feeling Bad," though I'm not feeling bad at all,
I'm feeling quite good, because it's the transitions
I've always loved, that sense of being
two places at once and in neither one,
the music taking me all the way out and back
to this car with Julie driving and behind us
our son and daughter sitting in the back seat
laughing at me rocking to the music, saying
"Daddy, can we have our silly glasses back?"

WHEREVER YOU ARE

When I kissed you in the hall
of the youth hostel we fell
into the linen closet laughing
twenty years ago and I still
remember though not very often
the taste of cheap wine in your mouth
like raspberries the freckle
between your breasts and the next day
when we went to Versailles I hardly
saw anything because I was looking
at you the whole time your face I can't
quite remember then I kissed you
good-bye and you got on a train
and I never saw you again just
one day and one letter long gone
explaining never mind but sometimes
I wonder where you are probably
married with children like me happy
with a new last name a whole life
having nothing to do with that day
but everybody has something like it
a small thing they can't help
going back to and it's not even about
choices and where your life might
have gone but just that it's there

far enough away so it can be seen
as just something that happened almost
to someone else an episode from
a movie we walk out of blinded
back into our lives

REMEMBERED DEPARTURE

Suddenly realizing it's been over a decade,
I think back to what it felt like to be going—
the plane shuddering down the runway, roaring with effort,
then finally tilting up and lifting off,
the gravity of our decision to leave for a year
trying to pull us back through the seats.
But soon we were cruising at 30,000 feet,
and by the time we crossed the International Date Line,
we felt almost weightless with the thought
that a whole day and all we'd left behind
had slipped beyond the horizon. What a relief!
We'd sentenced everything that had become our lives
to a year's confinement in a small dark cell,
never thinking what it would be like
to go back and find it there, smelling of must,
weighted down with all we had to do
to put it in order, a fist-sized generator
of panic kicking on in the pit of my stomach,
its hum of dread the soundtrack of my first
months back. But that was a year away,
and years ago. Since then we've made a life
that would be impossible to leave
even if we wanted to. Which might be why
I still look fondly back on that departure
when the only engines humming were the plane's

above the blue Pacific, our only baggage
what we could carry, nothing to declare.
Like the glossy items in the airport shops
we walked past after landing in Narita,
we were *duty free*, a phrase suddenly
lifted from its context, as we ourselves
had been. We were like an English expression
eagerly waiting to be transformed
and given new life by the Japanese:
chicken soap, navy green, I rub you.

SALT

I'm not sure when it started,
    the family tradition
        of using kosher salt,

coarse grains pinched
    between forefinger and thumb
        then held above our plates

and sprinkled down like snow
    on meat, potatoes, carrots.
        I didn't even know

what kosher meant
    until I was older,
        the six-pointed star

on the package was not yet
    a symbol of any kind,
        only a star of special interest

because it was made
    ingeniously of two
        triangles superimposed.

I had never eaten
        or even heard of bagels
                until I got to college,

where my neighbors
        in the dorm had names
                like Immerman, Perlstein,

Adelman, and Platnik.
        They had mezuzahs
                on their doorframes

like strange doorbells.
        Michael Chuback,
                a few doors down the hall,

had a pennant on his wall
        emblazoned with the words
                YESHIVA OF FLATBUSH,

a phrase so alien to me
        it might have been the name
                of a Hindu deity.

They teased me
        for being a WASP,
                but also took me in,

took me to their homes
        in Queens or New Jersey,
                where their parents

said things like, "I can't
        believe it: a goy in my house"
                and told me stories

of how *their* parents
        escaped the Gestapo
                or didn't, of growing up

on the Lower East Side,
        whole families in one room,
                stories that left me

speechless, feeling as if
        I had no history
                to speak of.

And then I fell in love
     with you, the heir
          of Lithuanian Jews,

drawn first by the beauty
     of your eyes—
          mildly exotic

yet instantly familiar,
     suggesting a world
          unknown to me

but which I longed
     to return to. And there
          I have remained, through all

the changes in our lives,
     the history we've
          created together.

Now, in a new house again,
     I sprinkle kosher salt
          in the corners of the rooms

as a Jewish friend of ours
            instructed me to do—
                        an old tradition

to ward off evil spirits—
            the salt of my childhood
                        and that of your ancestry

mingling in this
            partly ridiculous
                        partly sacred act.

ROWING

How many years have we been doing this together,
me in the bow rowing, you in the stern
lying back, dragging your hands in the water—
or, as now, the other way around, your body
moving toward me and away, your dark hair swinging
forward and back, your face flushed and lovely
against the green hills, the blues of lake and sky.

Soon nothing else matters but this pleasure,
your green eyes looking past me, far away,
then at me, then away, your lips I want to kiss
each time they come near me, your arms that reach
toward me gripping the handles as the blades
swing back dripping, two arcs of droplets
pearling on the surface before disappearing.

Sometimes I think we could do this forever,
like part of the vow we share, the rhythm
we find, the pull of each stroke on the muscles
of your arched back, your neck gorged and pulsing
with the work of it, your body rocking
more urgently now, your face straining with something
like pain you can hardly stand—then letting go,

the two of us gliding out over the water.

II

THE BURNING HAT

Whatever grief my parents felt
was lost on me, or is lost to me now.
But I do remember the Panama hat
that they brought back from the apartment
of Whoever-It-Was (a great-great-aunt?)
and gave to me. All afternoon I wore it
(despite the way it fell over my eyes),
pretending I was in a far-off country
where the hat brim fended off the sun
that blazed all day, even in winter.
I finally took it off at dinnertime,
placing it beside me on the bench
where I sat with my back to the fire.
The next thing I remember is how it fell
into the fireplace, and how it felt
to see it blaze up with the sound
of a great wind: unbearable. I reached
for the flames, then, through a blur of tears,
saw something amazing: the hat began to shrink—
smaller and smaller, yet holding its shape,
until I thought it was going to disappear
and screamed for it to stop. It stopped.
And there it was, more precious than before,
a perfect hat for a doll or puppet—too small for me
but longed for all the more. The flames

had died; a few small sparks crawled over it
with icy tinkling sounds. I held my breath,
then let it out again in a mournful sob
when that ghostly hat broke into ashes.

THREE WISHES

For Tom and Celeste McGraw

When they had to sell their place in Maine
and he was about to drive up one last time,
they told their three children they could each name
one final thing for him to bring back
from the house they'd spent so many summers in.

The oldest spoke first. She said: the curtains
in the living room—a gingham plaid
that had faded badly but would always
remind her of the time they'd spent
reading or playing Scrabble in that room.

The boy asked for the bone-handled hunting knife
left in the barn by the previous owners.
For years he'd seen it there, with its stained, curved blade,
but been afraid to take it, and afraid
until now even to say he wanted it.

When they turned to the youngest, she gave them
a fleeting, injured look with her dark eyes,
then seemed about to speak, but hesitated.
"What is it?" they asked, and she went over to them
and whispered, "The apple tree in the back yard."

He thought about that on the three-hour drive.
Alone at the house, he took down the curtains
and neatly folded them. On the way to the barn,
he stared a minute at the apple tree
she'd loved to climb. The hunting knife was gone.

VIETNAM SCRAPBOOK

Midway through fourth grade, early 1968,
Mrs. Hackemeyer said it was time
we learned about the war in Vietnam,
where, she said, "American boys
are giving their lives to fight communism."
We were American boys, or half of us were,
and we already knew communism was bad,
how it spread like a rash across the map
that pulled down like an illustrated window shade.

The paper maps that Mrs. Hackemeyer passed out
were scented with her perfume and showed a country
shaped vaguely like a sea horse, its slender waist
adorned with a slim, candy-striped belt
we labeled *DMZ*. We added stars and dots
and printed in *Saigon, Hanoi, Khe Sanh,
the Gulf of Tonkin, the Mekong River, Hue—*
names so strange they seemed to come
from an Asian version of *The Hobbit,*

which the librarian was reading aloud to us
in daily installments. Ho Chi Minh
might have been the leader of the evil goblins.
It was another world with its own vocabulary words—
"Charlie," chopper, napalm, punji—

words we lobbed like make-believe hand grenades
during recess, among our screams
of phony agony, our diving death-sprawls.
POWs were thrown into the Jungle Gym.

But they all escaped as soon as the bell rang,
the dead sprang up and ran inside
where Mrs. Hackemeyer tried to teach us
"the horror of war." *Horror* meant Godzilla,
and *Viet Cong* reminded us of King Kong.
Horror made you munch your popcorn faster.
Even after we started pasting photographs
from *Time* and *Life* into our notebooks—a task
that lasted weeks—it never broke through.

We clipped the jungle's blooming fireballs
with safety scissors, smeared minty paste
on the screaming napalm victim's back,
pressed the blood- and mud-spattered soldiers
into clean white pages, a little ink
smudging off on our soft, sticky fingertips,
as Mrs. Hackemeyer leaned over us
in her thick, invisible cloud of perfume,
smoke from bombed cities rising up in black plumes.

GOLDEN RETRIEVER

. . . bounding again into those childhood fields
with the dumb trust that nothing found in them
can hurt you. How long can this willed
innocence go on? Endlessly, it seems,
as long as you can make yourself believe
the world loves you. It's an old trick:
no matter how many times the stick
is thrown into the past, those days come back
drenched in the slobber of nostalgia.
Some dogs will go on fetching like that
until they literally drop dead
from exhaustion, faithful to the end—
but not to the way things really happened.
It's all the result of selective
memory, sniffing out the Golden Moments
while ignoring the carpet's yellow stains,
emblems (don't you remember?) of the shame
you were made to feel when your snout was thrust
in the puddle of urine or pile of shit
and a hand beat you. Shouldn't those primal scenes
be replayed, too? Forget the fucking stick.
Go find something really putrid to roll in
and smear all over your golden fur. Go on.

ANOTHER STORY

As soon as I began to show
the brooding signs of puberty—stubborn silences
broken by a forced and scornful laugh—
they moved me up to that attic room
where, in winter, I listened to the pipes
grumbling with my father's vexed inflection
but in a language I didn't understand,
and in summer a giant window fan
drowned out all utterance from the house below
and vented the suffocating heat,
pulling a cool wind up that extra flight
of stairs so I could breathe.

It was an exile I came to need.
Those gothic windows suited me,
dead wasps collecting behind cracked panes
like scarabs. I used to line them up
according to the angle of their spread wings,
a diagram for imaginary flights.
Above my desk, a map of the world
sagged from thumbtacks: some day
I would travel to countries far away.
Between one of Turner's fiery sunsets
and Hokusai's wave breaking in claws of foam,
Baudelaire stared out with tenebrous eyes.

Still, I had to eat. The odors of supper
tugged at my stomach and I trudged
down to the kitchen, where my father,
pouring bourbon over bursting cubes,
greeted me by telling me I looked
as pale as the celery in my mother's stew.
"Nice simile," I said sarcastically.
He'd make some teasing remark
about my "artsiness," and then I'd torch
the corporate world and ignite
an argument's exploding fireball,
whose pall of ashes settled over the meal.

But up there I was free to sulk and muse.
I thought Joyce's "Araby" was about me,
and when I read Auden's introduction
to Shakespeare's sonnets, I knew
that what I felt for the girl whose buoyant voice,
flushed complexion and least gesture obsessed me
was not a "crush" but a "Vision of Eros."
I never so much as touched her. Sex
was a minor eternity away. Meanwhile,
I bought a drab green, sweet and spicy cube of hash
wrapped in foil, and smoked it in that firetrap,
and laughed myself ridiculously happy.

MASTURBATION

One day we came upon it in the woods:
a snake swallowing a frog. Enthralled,
we stared at the slow horror of that devouring.
Later that summer, we caught a garter snake
and kept it in the window well of a cellar,
meeting there each afternoon for two weeks
to feed it frogs or toads. We could never get
enough of it: the way the snake unhinged its jaw
to take the frog in whole, gorging itself,
the beads of its eyes glinting in serious pleasure,
the frog kicking in desperation, twitching
in spasms, going rigid, then limp, the lump
moving endlessly down the snake's thickening length.
We urged it on each time, consumed by this secret
we shared, this sin we couldn't help going
back to, over and over—until one of our fathers
found us there and bellowed in disgust,
grabbed the snake by its yellow tail and flung it
into the woods it had come from, the woods
we'd return to, despite the shame that stung us.

SMOKE FOLLOWS BEAUTY

(traditional saying)

we used to say, standing around a campfire roasting
    marshmallows,
or, a little older, sitting and telling stories, laughing,
or listening to a guitar, some of us singing, others just staring
into the flames—until one of us got up and moved away,
hands rubbing eyes, then dodged to one side, fanning the
    smoke away,
and it was then that someone would say, "Smoke follows beauty,"
and whoever it was standing there would smile through tears.

We said it without thinking, without knowing where the saying
came from, or what it seemed to be saying: that there was no use
trying to get away, the smoke would follow you
away from the fire and into the night, and into the next day,
and through all the days of your life, shadowing your years,
until one day you succumbed to its smudged touch,
the pungent smell it leaves on your skin, and to tears.

THE DIVER

We hawked and spat into our masks, slipped on our flippers,
gripped the rubber mouthpiece of the snorkel in our teeth,
and swam out, peering into the lake's green interior,
each enclosed in the cocoon of his own breathing...
and in our different lives: he was a local
with a hick accent I mimicked behind his back,
I one of the privileged summer residents
he resented. Yet we were friends, bound together
by our seasonal crush on the same girl
and this almost daily ritual, the allure
of what mysterious treasures we might discover:
mostly old bottles, tossed off docks and boathouses
three generations back. Beer, whiskey, gin
and medicine bottles, seamless bottles of spun glass,
and old round-bottomed soda water bottles
of aquamarine glass, thick and full of bubbles,
like objects formed from the lake's own water
under the pressure and icy temperature
of depths we could hardly reach in one breath.

We used to scare ourselves with talk about "the bends"
and nitrogen narcosis, names which, with their tang
of death, we loved to say, though we were in no danger
kicking down through the thermocline, ears squeaking
on the eerie frequency of that submarine twilight

as we reached into the bottom's murk in search of something
worth bringing to light. Later, it became his life:
frogman in the army, then in a diving business.
He was behind the wheel of his pickup when the embolism
hit his brain—no chance for him to take a breath
before going under that last time, and yet the depth
was too much to fathom when I imagined him
down there, as in the old days: always outlasting me,
his skin glowing faintly with an unreal whiteness
when I took one final look at him in the dim light
before rushing up in a cloud of mushrooming bubbles
toward the mirrory underside of the surface,
legs furiously pumping as my lungs collapsed—
then plunging into daylight with a violent gasp.

THE OVAL PIN

sits on your dresser,
a gift a friend brought back from Russia:
a troika painted on black lacquer.

The three horses, one plunging forward,
one rearing up, one looking back
at the man and woman in the sleigh,

have some traditional significance
(she must have told you the story)
that you no longer remember.

You sense some urgency
in the way the man raises his whip
high, like the slimmest gold banner,

in the anxious expression
the artist managed to portray
on the woman's minuscule face,

and in the blanket or shawl
that trails and flaps behind the sleigh
like a twisted cloud of green smoke—

or almost like a shrouded body.
Something is wrong. A friend is ill
and dying. They must hurry.

But though the horses gallop wildly
like mythical beasts, with coats
of orange and pink and manes of flame,

though the sleigh lifts up and flies
through the night as black as lacquer,
these two on their dire errand

will never arrive in time to see
their friend alive, to say good-bye—
as we will never see again

the friend who gave you
this oval pin, which you reach for now
and fasten to your black dress.

(Ann Rubin, 1962–1998)

FIGURE

(Edward Anderson Woods, 1896–1998)

It almost seemed he'd just go
on and on, passing a hundred
then a hundred and one.
But though we were given
more than the usual
allotment to know him,
when he was gone
(suddenly, after so long),
we saw how little we knew:
his almost emaciated frame,
his reserved demeanor
from another era,
his wit as dry
as the gin he drank
earlier in the afternoon
as the years went by.
We could never quite get
at what was going on
behind his ample forehead.
He had served
in both World Wars
but never spoke of them.
And though his life spanned
the 20th Century,
it was ancient history

he knew by heart—
he barely seemed a part
of ours, practicing
a form of detachment
that was half a luxury,
a habit of lovely
evasive maneuvers,
and half a spareness
Buddhists might approve of.
He loved to dig up boulders
in the dirt road,
to clear brush and burn it
by the lake's shore,
feeding the fire
and staring into the flames.
But what did he see in them?
Did he have any demons,
or had he burned them away,
or cleansed himself of them
on his daily swim?
Wading into the lake,
he looked as skinny
as a Hindu ascetic
bathing in the Ganges,
immersing himself

without a splash
and breast-stroking out
into the sky's reflection.

WHITE SPACES

(Bert M-P. Leefmans, 1918-1980)

. . . hovering at the edges, elusive, he inhabits
spaces I would rather not clutter with words.

Even so, your words brought him back to me
and helped me find my own, remembering
that first day, when he lectured on Baudelaire
to five of us and a lot of empty seats,
speaking methodically, head in a cloud
of cigarette smoke, his frail hunched body
shuffling back and forth through a dust of ash.

He was not a romantic figure. More like
cut glass, chiseled, thin, emaciated, bent.

Soon we were meeting in his apartment
on Morningside, that street whose curving sweep
led us back to the turn of the century.
We pored over poems by Mallarmé,
surrounded by dozing snakes in glass cases
(he kept the mice to feed them in the kitchen).
He had a languid quality, like those snakes

—and something underneath, something like
the tautness of wire cutting down to truth—

working his way slowly through a poem
with a submerged urgency, examining
each word, while keeping all of them in view,
intent on any signalings between them.
"What matters is the relationship between
the words," he'd say, "and the spaces around them."
They wavered and swerved under our gaze,

   . . . shrugging and moving away, always on the move—
   he wouldn't or couldn't stay with his persona.

but as he spoke their oscillation slowed,
until the whole poem seemed to crystallize,
to hover free and luminous above the page.
But poetry was also bound to life
by words—he wanted us to see that, too—
a notion out of fashion among his colleagues,
who treated him as though his time had passed.

He knew about power and didn't want it.
He tore up almost everything he wrote.

I can almost hear him saying it's hopeless,
this effort to put him into words—both mine

and yours, who wish to go unnamed.
Your letter about him put me to shame.
You who knew him so much better than I did
saw the futility, though you went on
for three typed pages at the speed of passion:

He knew about beauty but wasn't possessive about it.
He knew about letting go of what he wanted.

One day when I revealed to him my dream
of writing "a whole new kind of poetry,"
he scolded me for "taking the wrong approach.
Just write the poems that come naturally.
Whether or not they're new is unimportant.
They have to come from you. Remember that."
I did, years later, but not in time to thank him.

. . . knowledge carried lightly, that nonchalance he kept
to the very end, when his heart was failing him.

I was too young and busy with my own life
even to notice he was sick, to be alarmed
by the cough that came from deep within his chest.
But one day my last semester, entering campus,

I saw the university's pale blue flag
at half-mast and instinctively changed course—
past Rodin's sullen *Thinker*, green with age,

An unconvinced survivor of his own life.
Le prince d'Aquitaine à la tour abolie.

into Philosophy, and up to his office door,
where a note explained he'd died the night before....
Gone now, known too briefly and too long ago
for me to bring him back in a poem,
though I'd like to think that what he was
and what he gave me hover at the edges
of these lines, in the white spaces around them

...always asking what can be found in words
and what forever lies beyond them.

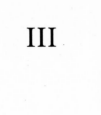

III

MEDUSA

(New England Aquarium)

Like fireworks, but alive,
a nebula exploding
over and over in a liquid sky,
this undulant soft bell
of jellyfish glowing orange
and trailing a baroque
mane of streamers, so
exquisite in its fluid
movements you can't pull
your body away, this lucent
smooth sexual organ
ruffled underneath
like a swimming orchid,
offers you a second–
hand ecstasy, saying
you can only get
this close by being
separate, you can only
see this clearly
through a wall of glass,
only imagine
what it might be like
to succumb to something
beyond yourself,
becoming nothing

but that pulsing,
your whole being reduced
to the medusa,
tentacled tresses flowing
entangled in a slow-motion
whiplash of rapture—
while you stand there,
an onlooker
turning to stone.

HORSESHOE CONTEST

(East Woodstock, Connecticut, Fourth of July)

After the parade
of tractors and fire trucks,
old cars and makeshift floats,
after speeches by
the minister and selectman,
after the cakewalk and hayrides
and children's games
are over and the cornet band
has packed up its instruments
and left the gazebo,
the crowd on the town
green begins to gather
around the horseshoe pit
where a tournament
has been going on all day
and is now down
to the four or five
best players—the same ones
every year, these old guys
who, beneath their feigned
insouciance, care about this
more than anything.
The stakes are high:
their name on a plaque,
their pride, their whole idea

of who they are,
held onto since high school
when they played football
or ran track—something
unchanging at their core,
small but of a certain heft.
Limber as gunslingers
preparing for a showdown,
they step up in pairs
to take their turns
pitching the iron shoes,
lofting these emblems
of luck with a skill
both deliberate and
offhand, landing ringer
after ringer, metal
clashing against metal,
while the others, those
who entered the contest
just for the hell of it
and who dropped out
hours ago, their throws
going wild or just
not good enough, stand
quietly at the sidelines,

watching with something close
to awe as their elders
stride with the casual
self-consciousness of heroes,
becoming young again
in the crowd's hush
and the flush of suspense,
elevated for these moments
like a horseshoe hanging
in the sunlit air
above them, above their lives
as dairymen and farmers,
their bodies moving
with a kind of knowledge
unknown to most of us
and too late for most of us
to learn—though I'd give
almost anything
to be able to do anything
that well.

NOT WRITTEN ON BIRCH BARK

When this afternoon
as I took my usual path
through fields and woods,
a patch of briars snatched
the poem from my hand,
I folded the paper up
and slipped it in my pocket,
trying for a while
to leave words behind.

But the world and the mind
work in funny ways,
for there on the path
ahead of me lay
a curled white page:
a strip of birch bark
whose native blankness
seemed to ask for words
but left nothing to say.

NECESSITY

John Clare
wrote poems
on scraps
of paper,

erased them
with bread
he ate
afterwards.

When he ran
out of scraps
he wrote
in his hat.

When he ran
out of bread
he ate
grass.

RILKE'S FEAR OF DOGS

had less to do
with any harm
they might inflict
than with the sad
look in their eyes
expressing a need
for love he felt
he couldn't meet.
And so he looked
away from them.

He was too busy
for such obligations,
waiting instead
for angels to speak,
looking up at heaven
with an expression
they couldn't help
responding to,
try as they might
to avoid his gaze.

SEX AND POETRY

(After a friend asked me why I didn't write more poems about sex)

For one thing, it's hard to get away with,
caught as we are red-handed in the Chamber
of Mimesis, one of those kinky rooms
with mirrors all over the walls and ceiling
where we hope to satisfy our unspeakable needs
but get instead an abyss of dwindling reflections.
Also, it's less like being in bed with a lover
than standing alone in front of a copy machine
Xeroxing her panties and bra. Snaps and garters
give way to the block and tackle of narrative,
which no amount of fumbling will undo.
Now tell me, does that sound like fun to you?

Sometimes, however, while we are looking
elsewhere, the green-gold dust of pollen falls
and begins to settle over everything
like an idea that takes over without our knowing
and adds a glow to whatever we see,
and we find ourselves in the middle of a sentence
we want to keep going, clause after clause,
as if the sinuosities of syntax were
the suave unfolding of limbs and skin
and language, a seduction to which we love
to succumb, feeling the words take shape in our mouths
and tasting them on someone else's tongue.

A GARBAGE CAN IN BROOKLYN
FULL OF BOOKS

Schweitzer, *The Teaching of Reverence for Life*.
Tich Nhat Hanh, *The Miracle of Mindfulness*.
Mortimer Adler, *Ten Philosophical Mistakes*.
John Stuart Mill in the familiar
formal attire of a Penguin Classic.
A few with *psychoanalysis* in the titles.

I see how it might get tiresome to have such titles
imploring you day after day to change your life.
It could easily plunge you into the classic
cycle of guilt and self-improvement, mindfulness
followed by depression, each glance at those familiar
spines reminding you of all the mistakes

you've made in the past, and the mistakes
to come. Who wouldn't want to clear the titles
from the shelves and return to the familiar
routine of a comfortable life
undisturbed by thought? A blissful mindlessness.
Throw away every last unread classic

(there's no such thing as a classic
anyway, they now say). Look, the whole mess takes
up only one can, though to undeniable fullness.

But wait. Digging down, I find the serious titles
have risen to the top like cream, or like the life–
preservers they're supposed to be (familiar

wisdom hauling us back up to the familiar
from uncertain depths). Or else these classics
have been placed on top deliberately, as if life
depended on concealing our...mistakes?
No, just dozens of trash novels flaunting bold titles
and heroines with breasts of unreal fullness—

like the fantasies our minds are full of,
hidden by good intentions—sound familiar?
What is this bizarre collection of titles
(quasi-porno side-by-side with classics)
but the unfinished, bound-to-be-full-of-mistakes
bibliography of someone's inner life?

THE POND OF DESIRES

... most desires end up in stinking ponds. . . .

—Auden

The water, if you can call it that, is black
as tar, and the lily pads are seared at the edges,
curling up as if trying not to touch it
more than they have to. The lilies themselves have gone
to seed, their pure white petals only a memory,
like the bass that used to cruise in the shadows.
The only fish left are suckers, kissing the same muck
that a lone duck upends itself to peck at:
so there must be some nourishment yet in these
jettisoned desiderata. Somewhere down there
is your brief, secret crush on a student,
the time you came within a kiss's width
of seduction, fantasies you hardly notice
yourself having before letting them sink
into this stinking pond. Slowly it fills up
and thickens into a swamp, where, some nights,
during the bullfrogs' lewd reverberations,
the effluvium bubbling up through the ooze
flickers elusively with a bodiless light.

INTERVAL

Sometimes, out of nowhere, it comes back,
that night when, driving home from the city,
having left the nearest streetlight miles behind us,

we lost our way on the back country roads
and found, when we slowed down to read a road sign,
a field alive with the blinking of fireflies,

and we got out and stood there in the darkness,
amazed at their numbers, their scattered sparks
igniting silently in a randomness

that somehow added up to a marvel
both earthly and celestial, the sky
brought down to earth, and brought to life,

a sublunar starscape whose shifting constellations
were a small gift of unexpected astonishment,
luminous signalings leading us away

from thoughts of where we were going
or coming from, the cares that often drive us
relentlessly onward and blind us

to such flickering intervals when moments
are released from their rigid sequence
and burn like airborne embers, floating free.

THE CARDINAL FLOWER

After an afternoon
of no fish, no strikes, nothing
rising for the fly
you tied yourself
out of deer hair, squirrel tail,
and turkey feathers,
you begin to give up,
your attention drifting
on the river's rippled skin,
along its bubbling eddies,
down the spillways between
boulders rusted orange,
and into pools shot through
with sun, like amber beer.
You wouldn't mind one now,
and you start back,
working your way along
a rocky shoal the river
has strewn with still puddles
filmed with silver-blue
iridescent mirrors.
Maybe you'll try to catch
the evening in watercolors,
exchanging one bag
of supplies for another,

flies for fine-haired brushes
you'll dip in the very
river you're painting,
the reflected sunset like
the pink-fading-to-silver
stripe of a rainbow trout.
But that one too
is bound to get away,
the painting you imagine
always fading
into the one you put
on paper and will never
get right. And yet you like
to think of it as you
head home. And suddenly
there it is, startling you
with its scarlet blooms,
the cardinal flower
alone on the riverbank,
holding your gaze taut
as the hummingbird
its survival depends on,
one red touch of the brush
to focus the whole scene.

ARRANGEMENT

(Priscilla Harrison Connell, 1926–1997)

The flowers that thrive on the margins,
by the tracks and roadsides as we pass
on our way somewhere else,
planted by no one and often unnoticed,
their beauty gratuitous, prodigal,
have nothing to do with us,
have nothing to do with decoration
but with survival.

　　　　　You survived
seven years after the diagnosis
and always noticed them, even when
you grew too weak to go out among them
in the early hours with your Nikon,
looking for things that others
might not see otherwise: the spider
that sews a lightning bolt into its web,
the monarch probing a milkweed's globe.

Now at the end of summer we drive home,
umbels of Queen Anne's lace and yellow tassels
of goldenrod swaying in the wake of our passing
and yours. Loosestrife in profusion
spreads its purple fabric through the marshes
spiked with dead trees. An occasional mullein

stands like a spear thrust into the earth as a marker,
its hilt flecked with one or two small blooms . . .

. . . their presence alongside us so faithful
we can't help having the delusion
that they are there because we need them,
even though you wouldn't have believed it.
You didn't want a funeral or flowers,
but these I have gathered without breaking
a single stem, and I think you would allow me
to place them on your grave.

CAR RADIO

Alone on the highway, you're nowhere
and anywhere inside your car. Velocity
throws time out the window like a cigarette
that hits the road and explodes in sparks,
and this glass and steel sheath of speed
becomes a time machine whose control panel
is the digital radio. Pop oldies and
what they now call Classic Rock transport you
to high school dances in gyms and hotels,
rock concerts in hockey rinks, summer camp,
even the monkey bars on the playground.
Each song brings back a different time and place,
some of which you'd rather not revisit,
and much of the music is lousy, embarrassing,
but all you have to do is press the SEEK button
and you can escape to somewhere else:
an almost-forgotten sublet in a city
where you haven't lived for decades,
the rooftop of a Miami high-rise at night,
a restaurant on the other side of the world.
And then there are all those times in other cars,
and you feel the one you're in transmogrifying
into an old VW bug, a battered Ford van
during the epoch of eight tracks and FM converters,
a friend's souped-up Jeep, the monster station wagons

of the grade school car pool. Some songs hit you
with a surge of fervency almost as pure
as it used to be when you could briefly think
of your life as a movie with a good soundtrack,
singing along to it until you got hoarse.
You don't do that any more, you've lost
that dorky and impetuous intensity,
though sometimes you look down at the speedometer
and you're going 85, and certain songs
can almost make you weep for junior high
and the obsessive, hopeless crushes of that era.
It gets to be too much, though, too tiring,
memories fading in and out like stations,
each exerting its capricious, hankering demands
with no resolution, so in order to break the spell
of nostalgia you switch to a jazz station
at the far left of the dial, music that doesn't
tug unfairly at your emotions, that brings you back
to the present, to clouds streaking the blue sky
and a flock of starlings rising up and turning
all at once in flight like notes in harmony
or all those selves inside you coming together.

THE AUTHOR

Richard Linke

Jeffrey Harrison is the author of two previous books of poetry, *The Singing Underneath*, selected by James Merrill for the National Poetry Series, and *Signs of Arrival*. He has received fellowships from the John Simon Guggenheim Memorial Foundation and the National Endowment for the Arts, as well as a Pushcart Prize, the Amy Lowell Traveling Poetry Scholarship, and the Lavan Younger Poets Award from the Academy of American Poets. His poems have appeared in *The New Yorker, The New Republic, Poetry, The Paris Review, The Yale Review*, and in many other magazines. He has taught at several universities, and at Phillips Academy, where he was the Roger Murray Writer-in-Residence for three years.